When Fred The Snake Got Squished, And Mended

written by
Peter B. Cotton

illustrated by
Bonnie Lemaire

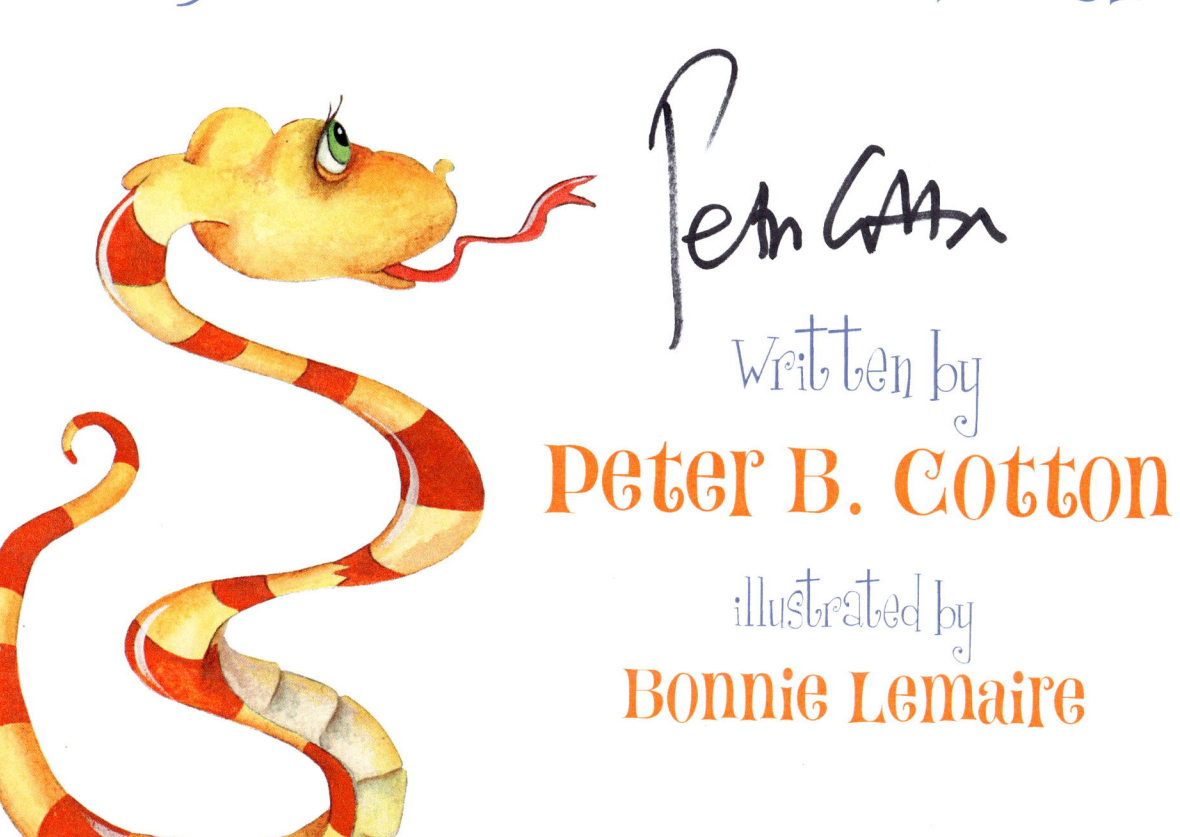

www.petercottontales.com

Second edition published 2018

Copyright © 2011 Peter B. Cotton

All rights reserved. No part of this book may be reproduced in any
form or by any electronic or mechanical means,
including information storage and retrieval systems,
without permission in writing from the publisher, except
by reviewers, who may quote brief passages in a review.

ISBN-13: 978-1-948543-42-2

Illustrations by Bonnie Lemaire
Cover and book design by Cdesign Graphics

Printed in the United States of America.

"Fred-Fred" was written many years ago for my children, Andrew and Nicola. It is now published and dedicated to their wonderful children, Alexandra, Charlotte, Isobelle, Perdita and Jack.

This Book Belongs To:

Leo

One day, as we sat down to tea,
a package came, addressed to me;
the sort with holes in it, which leave
air inside, for pets to breathe.

There, lying on a leafy bed
was my gift, a snake called Fred.
A note said "love from Jungle Jim
be sure and take good care of him".

Fred was his name, but soon, instead,
we'll have to call him 'Fred-dash-Fred'
for I'll tell you how we made ends meet
when he lost his head while crossing the street.

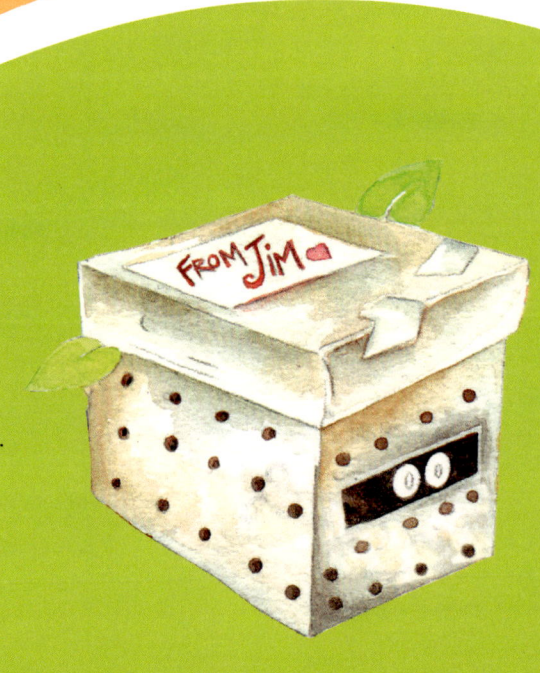

Fred came from a steamy forest spot
where even winter days are hot
the home of hairy beasts that go oink-oink
and drop things on your head, boink-boink.

It's a swampy place with lots of squelch
the only noise a muffled belch
of a nearby rhino in the mud
chewing the primeval cud.

Such a rush when we first went out
with noise and cars all dashing about.

Fred was jungle-trained a treat
but, could he cross a busy street?

When we came to cross the road
Fred quite forgot his Forest Code.

He thought the barber's stripy pole
was a friendly snake, but, oh my soul

Fred dashed across with never a glance
into the path of an ambulance.

With a horrible SCREECH, it wasn't his fault
the driver did his best to halt
and, like most snakes
Fred had no brakes.

Before my eyes poor hurrying Fred
was CUT IN TWO...he scarcely bled
for in snakes blood a something flows
to stop them leaking when they're squoze.

The driver jumped down, from his pack he took
his first-aid kit and his first-aid book —
in the index found "for SNAKES DIVIDED
use the longest splint provided."

But even that was much too small
The two Fred parts were far too tall.

We had to call for further aid
and pretty soon the Fire-Brigade
had Fred all comfy on their ladder
(they'd once been called to a fractured adder).

With Police cars leading them ahead
they dashed through all the lights at red
and halted at the Hospital gate.
Oh, will they have to operate?

Doctors came and called a Vet
not a case they often get.
They sounded his chest and made him sick
by poking his throat with a long flat stick.
They put him on trolleys (he needed four)
and wheeled him through the X-Ray door.

I saw the specialist doctor frown
as he put poor Fred-Fred's X-rays down.
"We'll have to do our best to sew
these ends together, but you know
(to the nurses gathered round he said)
I'll need a special sort of thread
full of twist and curl and bend
to make a proper snake-proof mend.

This thread comes only from the leaf
of a certain bush which grows beneath
large rhinos. But, who will dare
disturb that wild beast in his lair?"

"Volunteers, please give your names."

Suddenly I thought of James
who enjoys, so one supposes,
hunting fierce Rhi-nos-cer-oses.

So we wrote post-haste to Jim
in CATIPALS, informing him
of the needs of Fred, or rather Freds,
for the parts now lay in separate beds.

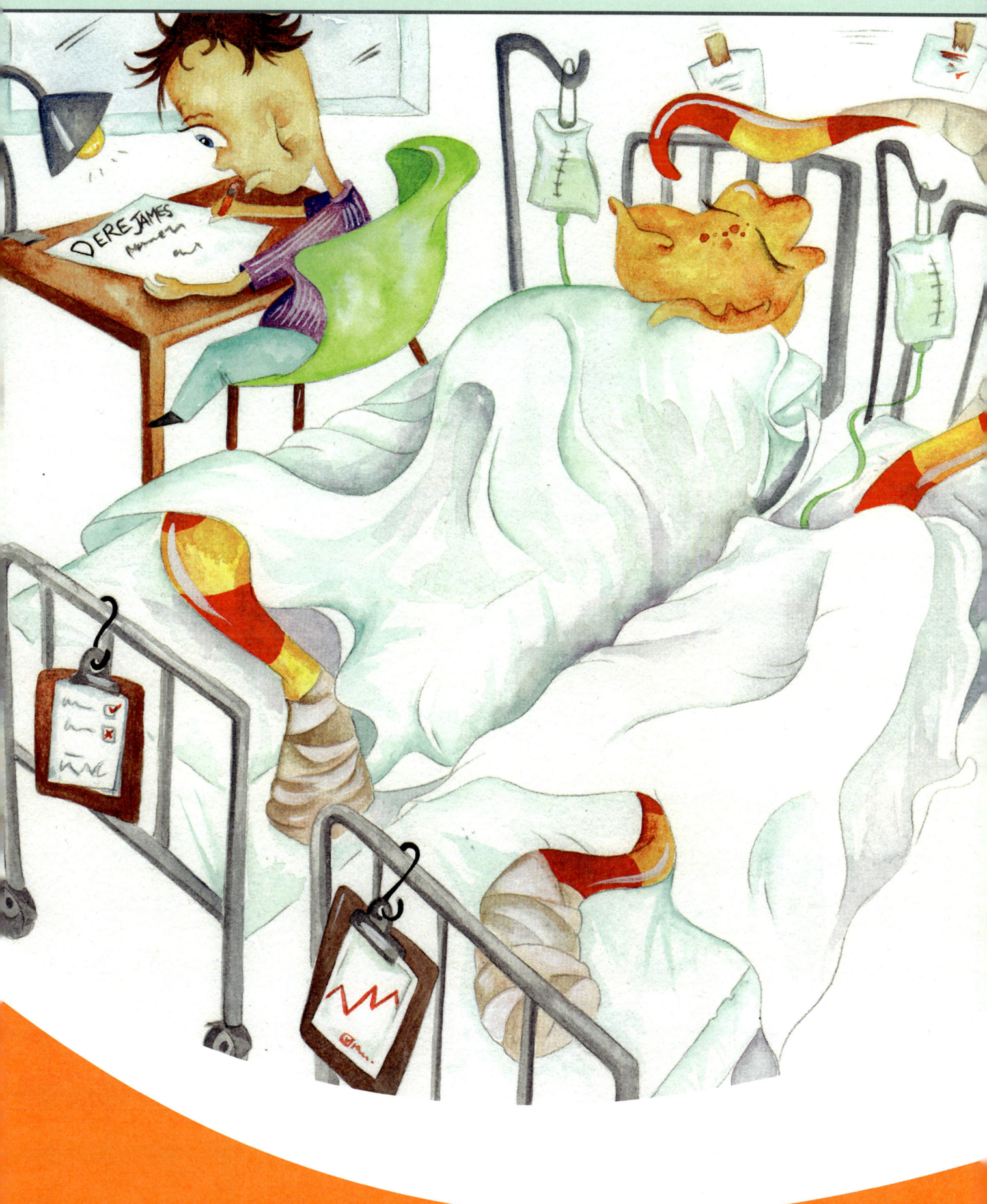

Jim read the note, but his mortal dread
was waking rhinos in their beds.

But he bravely started out to hike
(he'd punctured his exploring bike)
and laid his bait, an open box
of rhino's favourite sort of chocs.

Woken from his dreamy coma
by a birthday sort aroma
the rhino staggered to his feet
and shambled off towards his treat.

From his hiding-place, neck-deep in slime
Jim, picking the auspicious time
stretched out his hand and with it caught
the leaf our Fred-Fred's doctor sought.

With loving care he packed it in
his jungle-issue sandwich tin
and sealed it with a Forest stamp.

A monkey swung it back to camp
and sent it seagull-post that day
across the seas where Fred-Fred lay.

The doctor then, immediately
or, rather, when he'd had his tea,
prepared the thread and started sewing
Fred-Fred's coming to his going.

The brave snake didn't cry or ouch
on the operating couch.

Then doctor asked the nurse to bring
the special snakey sort of sling
which helps in bendy types of healing.
Soon Fred was slung up from the ceiling!

Within a week, with stitches out
Fred found that he could twist about.
He did his exercises so
they soon pronounced him fit to go.

Fred kept a careful hold of me
as we hurried home for tea
of jelly, cream, and beans on toast
the things that mended Freds like most.

Then we wrote brave Jim a letter
saying Fred was so much better
and thanked him for the jungle trip
to provide our snake with a sort of zip.

Then Fred washed, put on his jamas-
just the leg part, not the armas-
and curled up, having said his prayers
in his box beneath the stairs.

As he fell asleep I heard Fred say
"It's been a very trying day.
Tomorrow, when I'm on the road
I won't forget my Crossing Code."

And nor will you, that's my advice
Lest you spell your name like Fred-Fred twice.

Peter Cotton was born in Herefordshire, England, where his father was a country physician. He was educated at Cambridge University and St. Thomas's Hospital Medical School (London) and became a doctor in 1963. He specialized in digestive problems (gastroenterology). After running a department at The Middlesex Hospital in London for 12 years he moved to Duke University in North Carolina as Professor of Medicine and Chief of Endoscopy in 1986. He moved again in 1994 to found the Digestive Disease Center at the Medical University of South Carolina in Charleston. He remains there part-time in research and teaching. He published his medical memoirs, *The Tunnel at the End of the Light: My Endoscopic Journey in Six Decades*, in 2010.

The first Fred story, *When Fred the Snake Got Squished, and Mended* was written for his then young children, to teach them how not to cross the road. When in turn they had their own children, they asked "What happened to Fred-Fred?" That stimulated publication, with the help of an excellent illustrator, Bonnie Lemaire. There are now five popular and award-winning books about Fred the Snake.

Feel free to visit the website **www.petercottontales.com**, where you will learn that Peter was not named after a rabbit.

The four other books about Fred the friendly snake...

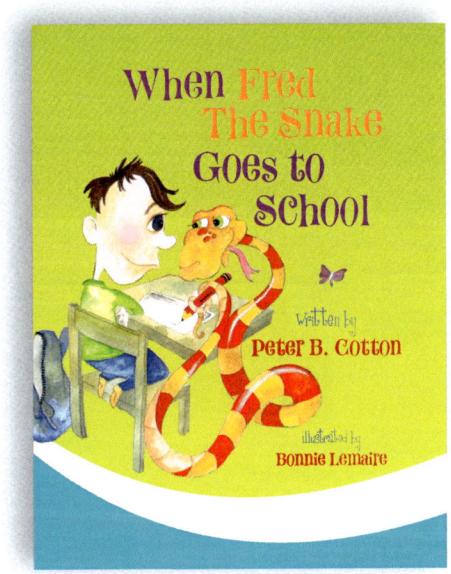

When Fred The Snake Goes to School
PAPERBACK: 978-1-948543-45-3
HARDBACK: 978-1-948543-46-0
eBOOK: 978-1-948543-47-7

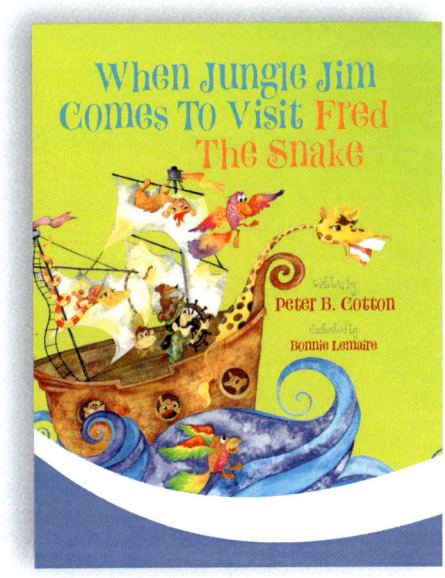

When Jungle Jim Comes to Visit Fred The Snake
PAPERBACK: 978-1-948543-48-4
HARDBACK: 978-1-948543-49-1
eBOOK: 978-1-948543-50-7

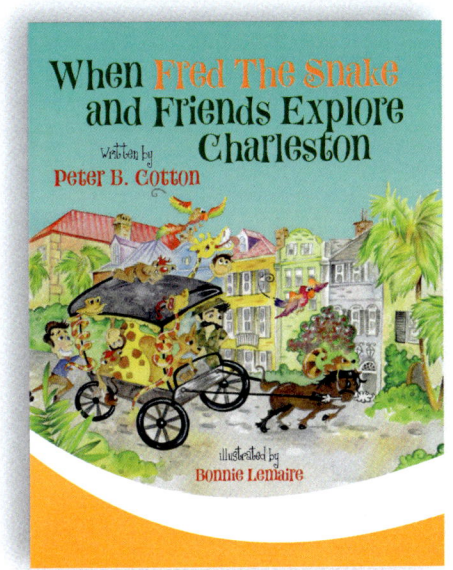

When Fred The Snake and Friends Explore Charleston
HARDBACK: 978-0-692570-72-2

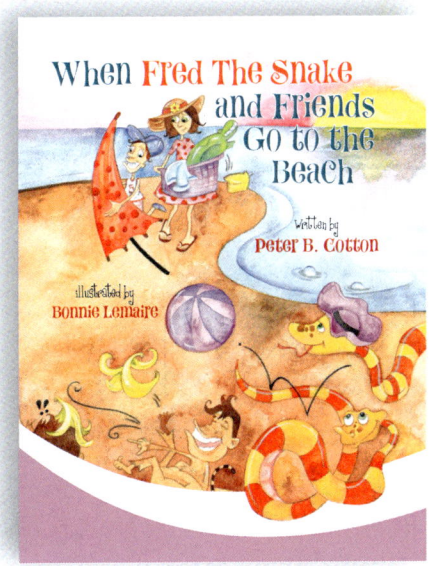

When Fred the Snake and Friends Go to the Beach
HARDBACK: 978-1532343-00-1

AVAILABLE AT AMAZON AND BOOK STORES.
Signed copies available at www.petercottontales.com.

Made in the USA
Lexington, KY
28 September 2018